شرح كتاب فضل الإسلام

للإمام المجدد شيخ الإسلام محمد بن عبد الوهاب

شرحه الإمام عبد العزيز بن عبد الله بن باز

Explanation of the Superiority of Islaam

Written by

Shaykh ul-Islaam Muhammad bin 'Abdul Wahhaab

Explained by

Al-Imaam 'Abdul 'Azeez bin 'Abdullaah bin Baaz

permissions@ibnulqayyim.com
Ibnul Qayyim Publications

www.ibnulqayyim.com
Phone: +1-214-329-1238
Fax: +1-214-447-9549

ISBN 0-9752953-0-6

First edition: May 2005
Printed In Canada

Table of Contents

With the name of Allaah, the Most Merciful, the Bestower of Mercy

The superiority of Islaam

Allaah the Exalted says,

﴿ ٱلْيَوْمَ أَكْمَلْتُ لَكُمْ دِينَكُمْ وَأَتْمَمْتُ عَلَيْكُمْ نِعْمَتِى وَرَضِيتُ لَكُمُ ٱلْإِسْلَـٰمَ دِينًا ﴾

"This day, I have perfected your religion for you, completed My Favor upon you, and have chosen for you Islaam as your religion." *Al-Maa'idah (5):3*

And Allaah says,

﴿ قُلْ يَـٰٓأَيُّهَا ٱلنَّاسُ إِن كُنتُمْ فِى شَكٍّ مِّن دِينِى فَلَآ أَعْبُدُ ٱلَّذِينَ تَعْبُدُونَ مِن دُونِ ٱللَّهِ وَلَـٰكِنْ أَعْبُدُ ٱللَّهَ ٱلَّذِى يَتَوَفَّىٰكُمْ ﴾

"Say (O Muhammad (ﷺ)): 'O you mankind! If you are in doubt as to my religion (Islaam), then (know that) I will never worship those whom you worship besides Allaah. But I worship Allaah Who causes you to die.'" *Yoonus (10):104*

Allaah also says,

﴿ يَـٰٓأَيُّهَا ٱلَّذِينَ ءَامَنُوا۟ ٱتَّقُوا۟ ٱللَّهَ وَءَامِنُوا۟ بِرَسُولِهِۦ يُؤْتِكُمْ كِفْلَيْنِ مِن رَّحْمَتِهِۦ وَيَجْعَل لَّكُمْ نُورًا تَمْشُونَ بِهِۦ وَيَغْفِرْ لَكُمْ ۚ وَٱللَّهُ غَفُورٌ رَّحِيمٌ ﴾

"O you who believe! Fear Allaah, and believe in His Messenger (Muhammad (ﷺ)). He will give you a double portion of His Mercy, and He will give you a light by which you shall walk (straight), and He will forgive you. And Allaah is Oft-Forgiving, Most Merciful." *Al-Hadeed (57):28*

In the *Saheeh* it is narrated from Ibn 'Umar that the Messenger of Allaah (ﷺ) said,

مثلكم ومثل أهل الكتابين كمثل رجل ا ستأجر أجيراً فقال: من يعمل لي من غدوة إلي نصف النهار على قيراط؟ فعملت اليهو د، ثم قال: من يعمل من نصف النهار إلى صلاة العصر على قيراط؟ فعملت النصارى، ثم قال: من يعمل من صلاة العصر إلى أن تغيب الشمس على قيراطين؟ فأنتم هم، فغضبت اليهو د والنصارى، وقالوا:

مالنا أكثر عملا وأقل أجرا؟ قال: هل نقصتكم من حقكم

شيئاً؟ قلوا: لا قال: ذلك فضلي أوتيه من أ شا ء

"The comparison between you all (the Muslims) and the people of the two Scriptures (the Jews and Christians) is like a man who seeks to hire a worker. He says, 'Who will work for me from morning until noon for one *qeeraat* (monetary unit)?' So the Jews worked. Then he says, 'Who will work for me from noon until the mid-afternoon ('Asr) prayer for one *qeeraat*?' So the Christians worked. Then he says, 'Who will work from the mid-afternoon prayer until the sun sets for two *qeeraat*?' So you all (the Muslims) are those (people). Thus, the Jews and Christians became angry and said, 'Why have we done more work but we have received less pay?' He (Allaah) replied, 'Have I decreased anything from what was rightfully yours?' They answered, 'No.' He then said, "That is My Favor which I give to whoever I wish.'"

It is also reported in the *Saheeh* from Abu Hurairah that the Messenger of Allaah (ﷺ) said,

أضل الله عن الجمعة من كان قبلنا، فكان لليهو د يوم

السبت، وللنصارى يوم الأحد، فجا ء الله بنا فهدانا ليوم

الجمعة، وكذلك هم تبع لنا يوم القيامة: نحن آخرون من أهل الدنيا والأولون يوم القيامة

"Allaah misguided those who were before us concerning *Jumu'ah* (Friday). The Jews had Saturday and the Christians had Sunday. Then Allaah brought us and He guided us to *Jumu'ah* (Friday). Likewise, they (the Jews and Christians) will be after us on the Day of Judgement. We are the last religious nation of the people of this world, but we will be the first on the Day of Judgement."

And in the *Saheeh* it is narrated that the Prophet said,

أحب الإيمان إلى الله الحنيفية السمحة

"The most beloved faith to Allaah is the tolerant *Haneefiyyah* (i.e. Islaamic Monotheism)."

It is reported from Ubayy bin Ka'b that he said, "You all must adhere to the Path and the *Sunnah*. For verily, there is no servant (of Allaah) who is upon the Path and the *Sunnah*, and who remembers Allaah, thus causing his eyes to overflow with tears due to fear of Allaah, except that the Fire (of Hell) will not touch him. And there is no servant (of Allaah) who is upon the Path and the *Sunnah* of the Most Gracious (Allaah), and his skin shivers due to fear of Allaah, except that he will be like a tree with leaves that have dried. His sins will fall from him just like the leaves of this tree fall from it. Verily, moderation in (following) the *Sunnah* is better than much effort (i.e. hard work) in opposing the Path and the *Sunnah*."

It is reported from Abu Ad-Dardaa' that he said, "How wonderful is the sleep and the eating of the intelligent ones. How is it that they criticize the wakeful vigilance and fasting of the foolish people?

"An atom's weight of righteousness with piety (fear of Allaah) and conviction is greater, more virtuous and better than the worship performed by those who are deceived (i.e. misguided people)." [1]

---

[1] The intent behind this is that Allaah, the Most High, made Islaam the best of all religions, and it is the religion of Allaah, which brings about happiness and salvation. And the servant (of Allaah), if he is upright upon Islaam, and he adheres to it, then he will have (as his reward) Paradise and honor. Also, the efforts of the servant (of Allaah) in his prayer and fasting, or other things besides that, if he does them upon other than the *Sunnah*, they do not benefit him. Allaah says (the English meaning is),

"This day, I have perfected your religion for you, completed My Favor upon you, and have chosen for you Islaam as your religion." *Al-Maa'idah (5):3*

And He says (the English meaning is),

"And whoever seeks a religion other than Islaam, it will never be accepted of him." *Aal 'Imraan (3):85*

Therefore, what is obligatory upon every responsible (i.e. sane, adult, Muslim) person is to adhere to Islaam and to strive to obey Allaah, the Most High. This is the path of happiness. So moderation upon Islaam and traversing upon its path with a small amount of actions is better than an abundance of effort and striving upon other than Islaam and the *Sunnah*. And there is no power or strength except with Allaah.

The obligation of accepting Islaam

Allaah says,

﴿ وَمَن يَبْتَغِ غَيْرَ ٱلْإِسْلَـٰمِ دِينًا فَلَن يُقْبَلَ مِنْهُ وَهُوَ فِى ٱلْـَٔاخِرَةِ مِنَ ٱلْخَـٰسِرِينَ ﴾

"And whoever seeks a religion other than Islaam, it will never be accepted from him, and in the Hereafter he will be one of the losers." *Aal-'Imraan (3):85*

Allaah also says,

﴿ وَأَنَّ هَـٰذَا صِرَٰطِى مُسْتَقِيمًا فَٱتَّبِعُوهُ ۖ وَلَا تَتَّبِعُوا۟ ٱلسُّبُلَ فَتَفَرَّقَ بِكُمْ عَن سَبِيلِهِۦ ﴾

"And verily, this is my Straight Path, so follow it, and follow not *As-Subul* (other paths), for they will separate you away from His path." *Al-An'aam (6):153*

Mujaahid said, "*As-Subul* (the paths) means the innovations and the doubtful matters."

It has been narrated from 'A'ishah that the Messenger of Allaah (ﷺ) said,

من أحدث في أمرنا هذا ما ليس منه فهو رد

"Whoever introduces into our affair (Islaam) that which is not from it, then it (his innovation) is rejected." (Agreed upon)

In another wording of this narration he said,

من عمل عملا ليس عليه أمرنا فهو رد

"Whoever performs any deed that our affair (Islaam) is not upon, then it (his deed) is rejected."

Al-Bukhaaree has narrated from Abu Hurairah that the Messenger of Allaah (ﷺ) said,

كل أمتي يدخلون الجنة إلا من أبى - قيل: ومن أبى؟ قال:

من أطاعني دخل الجنة ومن عصاني فقد أبى

"All of my *Ummah* (followers) will enter Paradise except for those who refuse." It was said, "And who would refuse?" He replied, "Whoever obeys me will enter Paradise, and whoever disobeys me, then he has refused (to enter Paradise)."

In the *Saheeh* it is narrated from Ibn 'Abbaas that the Messenger of Allaah (ﷺ) said,

أبغض الناس إلى الله ثلاثة: ملحد في الحرم، ومبتغ في الإسلام سنة الجاهلية، ومطلب دم امرئ مسلم بغير حق ليهريق دمه

"The most hated people to Allaah are three: a deviant (religious heretic) in the sanctuary of the Haram (Makkah), one who seeks to introduce the *sunnah* (way, tradition, custom) of pre-Islaamic ignorance (*Jaahiliyyah*) into Islaam, and the one who seeks to shed the blood of a Muslim man without the right to do so." (Al-Bukhaaree) [2]

Ibn Taymiyyah said, "His statement: 'the *sunnah* (way, tradition, custom) of pre-Islaamic ignorance,' all types of pre-Islaamic ignorance are included in this, restrictively or without restriction. This means that some aspects of it may be in some people and not others -- whether it is from the ways of the People of

---

[2] The point of proof here is his statement, **"And the one who seeks the way of pre-Islaamic ignorance (*Jaahiliyyah*) into Islaam."** And verily what is obligatory upon the servant of Allaah is to adhere to Islaam, while avoiding the ways of pre-Islaamic ignorance. So actions in Islaam, even though they may be few, is what will bring about benefit. In reference to striving that one makes upon ways other than Islaam, and other than the *Sunnah*, then that only harms and it does not benefit. Therefore, it is obligatory upon all responsible people (i.e. sane, adult, Muslims) to adhere to Islaam and restrict themselves to the religion of Allaah. They must traverse upon it (Islaam) in everything, with sincerity to Allaah and following the Messenger (ﷺ).

the Scripture (i.e. Christians and Jews), the ways of the idol worshippers, or other than them, from every type of opposition to what the Messengers came with."

It is narrated in the Saheeh that Huthayfah said, "O community of *Qurraa'* (reciters), [3] stand firm and upright (upon Islaam), [4] for verily you have advanced far ahead (of others). But if you deviate to the right or to the left, then you will have gone far astray."

---

[3] The *Qurraa'* (literally meaning reciters) here means the Scholars and the Students of Knowledge.

[4] And the meaning of his statement **"stand firm and upright"**, means upon the path. In other words, stand firm and be upright upon the religion of Allaah. So if the servant of Allaah stands firm, then indeed he will advance far ahead of others. And if he deviates to the right or to the left, then indeed he will go far astray. Thus, it is obligatory to adhere to what Allaah legislated, and to beware of whatever Allaah rebuked. Allaah said (the English meaning is),

> **"Or have they partners with Allaah (false gods) who have instituted for them a religion which Allaah has not ordained?"** *Ash-Shooraa (42):21*

So the matter of him being upon the path, even if it is moderate in amount, along with the righteous people and the people who do a moderate amount of deeds, that is better than him traversing upon paths that deviate away from right guidance, because they will lead him astray and take him away from Allaah, the Mighty and Majestic. Rather, the person of right guidance, even though he may oppress himself by committing some acts of disobedience, he is still upon the path of salvation. However, whoever traverses upon other than Islaam, and he desires the way of *Jaahiliyyah* in Islaam, then he is upon the path of destruction. We ask Allaah for safety and well-being.

It has been narrated from Muhammad bin Wadhdhaah that he used to enter the *masjid* and stand over the circles (of knowledge and learning), and he would say a word of admonition.

On one occasion he said, "Ibn 'Uyainah informed us from Mujaahid, who narrated from Ash-Sha'bee, who narrated from Masrooq who said that 'Abdullaah (Ibn Mas'ood) said, 'There is not a year except that the year after it is worse than it. Do not say that a year is more prosperous than another year, or a leader (*Ameer*) is better than another leader. For indeed, your Scholars and the best of you have passed away. Then there will come people who will begin to analyze matters according to their opinions, and thus Islaam will be destroyed and breached.'"

The explanation of Islaam

Allaah says,

﴿ فَإِنْ حَآجُّوكَ فَقُلْ أَسْلَمْتُ وَجْهِيَ لِلَّهِ وَمَنِ ٱتَّبَعَنِ ﴾

"So if they dispute with you (Muhammad (ﷺ)) say: 'I have submitted myself to Allaah (in Islaam), and (so have) those who follow me.'" *Aal 'Imraan (3):20*

It has been narrated in the *Saheeh* from Ibn 'Umar that the Messenger of Allaah (ﷺ) said,

الإسلام أن تشهد أن لا إله إلا الله، وأن محمدا رسول الله، وتقيم الصلاة، وتؤتي الزكاة، وتصوم رمضان، وتحج البيت إن استطعت إليه سبيلا

"Islaam is that you testify that none has the right to be worshipped but Allaah, and Muhammad is the Messenger of Allaah, you establish the prayer, you give the *Zakaah* (obligatory charity), you fast (the month of) *Ramadhaan*, and you make *Hajj* (pilgrimage) to the House (*Ka'bah*) if you are able to find a way there." [5]

---

[5] And this is the response of the Prophet (ﷺ) to Jibraa'eel when he asked him about Islaam. Thus, the Prophet (ﷺ) responded with this answer, just as it has

It is also narrated in the *Saheeh* from Abu Hurairah that the Prophet (ﷺ) said,

المسلم من سلم المسلمون من لسانه ويده

"The Muslim is he whom the Muslims are safe from his tongue and his hand." [6]

It is reported from Bahz bin Hakeem, who reported from his father, who reported from his grandfather that the Messenger of Allaah (ﷺ) was asked about Islaam. So he said,

---

come in the ***hadeeth*** of 'Umar, and this is the explanation of its pillars. And Islaam is broader than this (i.e. just these five pillars), as it includes whatever Allaah and His Messenger commanded, and it is to abandon whatever Allaah and His Messenger prohibited. Just as Allaah, the Most High, said (the English meaning is),

> **"Truly, the religion with Allaah is Islaam."** *Aal 'Imraan (3):19*

However, these are its pillars. For indeed a thing may be explained by its pillars, and it may be explained by all of its parts.

[6] **"The Muslim is he whom the Muslims are safe from his tongue and his hand."** This proves the broadness (of Islaam) and that Islaam is more comprehensive (than just the pillars). It includes the pillars and things other than the pillars as well. So the true Muslim, he is the one who performs the pillars and performs that which Allaah made obligatory upon him. He also refrains from oppressing people and transgressing the limits of Allaah.

أن تسلم قلبك لله، وأن تولي وجهك إلى الله، وأن تصلي الصلاة المكتوبة، وتؤتي الزكاة المفروضة

"It is that you submit your heart unto Allaah, and you turn your face to Allaah, and you pray the obligatory prayer (*Salaah*), and you give the prescribed *Zakaah* (obligatory charity)." (Ahmad)

Abu Qilaabah reported from 'Amr bin 'Abasah, who reported from a man from the people of Ash-Shaam (the area of Syria, Palestine and Jordan), who reported from his father that the Messenger of Allaah (ﷺ) was asked, "What is Islaam?" He replied,

أن تسلم قلبك لله ويسلم المسلمون من لسانك ويدك قال: أي الإسلام أفضل؟ قال: الإيمان قال: وما الإيمان؟ قال أن تؤمن بالله وملائكته وكتبه ورسله والبعث بعد الموت

"It is that you submit your heart unto Allaah, and that the Muslims are safe from your tongue and your hand." The questioner then said, "What Islaam is the best?" The Prophet (ﷺ) said, "Faith (*Al-Eemaan*)." The questioner then said, "What is faith?" The Prophet replied, "It is that you believe in Allaah, His Angels, His Books, His Messengers, and the Resurrection after death."

The statement of Allaah, the Most High, "And whoever seeks a religion other than Islaam, it will never be accepted from him." [7]

It has been narrated from Abu Hurairah that the Messenger of Allaah (ﷺ) said,

تجيء الأعمال يوم القيامة فتجيء الصلاة فتقول: يا رب أنا الصلاة فيقول: إنك على خير، ثم يجيء الصيام فيقول: إنك على خير، ثم تجيء الأعمال على ذلك فيقول: إنك على خير، ثم يجيء الإسلام فيقول: يا رب إنك السلام وأنا الإسلام فيقول: إنك على خير، بك اليوم آخذ وبك أعطى قال الله تعالى: ﴿ وَمَن يَبْتَغِ غَيْرَ ٱلْإِسْلَٰمِ دِينًا فَلَن يُقْبَلَ مِنْهُ وَهُوَ فِى ٱلْءَاخِرَةِ مِنَ ٱلْخَٰسِرِينَ ﴾

"The deeds will come on the Day of Judgement; so the prayer (*Salaah*) will come and say, 'O Lord! I am prayer (*Salaah*).' So Allaah will say, 'Verily, you are upon goodness.' The fasting will come and He

---

[7] The meaning of this is that it is obligatory upon all of the Islaamic *Ummah* and that there is no salvation for the *Ummah*, nor any happiness for it, except with Islaam.

(Allaah) will say, 'Verily, you are upon goodness.' Then the (other) deeds will come like that, and He (Allaah) will say, 'Verily, you are upon goodness.' Then Islaam will come and it will say, 'O Lord! Verily, you are *As-Salaam* (the one free of all faults) and I am Islaam.' So He (Allaah) will say, 'Verily, you are upon goodness. Today I will take (accept) because of you, and I will give (reward) because of you.' [8] Allaah the Most High says,

---

[8] **"Today I will take (accept) because of you, and I will give (reward) because of you."** So whoever dies upon Islaam, then he will have Paradise, either from the first *Wahlah* (stage of judgement) if he is safe from the sins, or after the punishment which Allaah has decreed upon him due to the sins that he died upon if Allaah does not pardon him. So there is no salvation except with Islaam. Allaah, the Most High, said (the English meaning is),

"And whoever seeks a religion other than Islaam, it will never be accepted of him." *Aal 'Imraan (3):85*

So whoever dies upon other than Islaam, even though he may have whatever he has of acts of obedience (i.e. good deeds) the size of mountains, verily those deeds will be lost. Allaah said (the English meaning is),

"And We shall turn to whatever deeds they (disbelievers, polytheists, sinners, etc.) did, and We shall make such deeds as scattered floating particles of dust." *Al-Furqaan (25):23*

There must be *At-Tawheed* by testifying that there is none worthy of worship except Allaah, and that Muhammad is the Messenger of Allaah. The person must enter Islaam with his heart and accept it, then after that, there must be actions. So whoever stands firm and upright upon actions, then he will enter the Paradise from the first *Wahlah* (stage of judgment), and whoever is deficient in anything from the actions that are obligatory upon him, or he commits some of the acts of

﴿ وَمَن يَبْتَغِ غَيْرَ ٱلْإِسْلَٰمِ دِينًا فَلَن يُقْبَلَ مِنْهُ وَهُوَ فِى ٱلْءَاخِرَةِ مِنَ ٱلْخَٰسِرِينَ ﴾

'And whoever seeks a religion other than Islaam, it will never be accepted of him, and in the Hereafter he will be one of the losers.' (*Aal 'Imraan (3):85*)" (Ahmad)

In the *Saheeh* it is narrated from 'A'ishah that the Messenger of Allaah (ﷺ) said,

من عمل عملا ليس عليه أمرنا فهو رد

"Whoever performs a deed that our affair (Islaam) is not upon, then it (his deed) is rejected." (Muslim and Ahmad)

---

disobedience (i.e. sins) which Allaah has forbidden, then he will be left to the will of Allaah. If Allaah wills He will pardon him, and if He wills He will punish him according to the amount of sins that he has with him. This is as Allaah, the Most High, said (the English meaning is),

"Verily, Allaah forgives not that partners should be set up with Him (in worship) but He forgives except that (anything else) to whom He pleases."
An-Nisaa' (4):48

So whoever Allaah guides to Islaam, and he is safe from committing *Shirk* (associating a partner with Allaah), then he is upon the path of salvation.

The obligation of being satisfied with following the Book besides everything other than it

Allaah says,

﴿وَنَزَّلْنَا عَلَيْكَ ٱلْكِتَـٰبَ تِبْيَـٰنًا لِّكُلِّ شَىْءٍ﴾

"And We have sent down to you the Book (the Qur'aan) as an exposition of everything." *An-Nahl (16):89*

An-Nasaa'ee and others have recorded that the Prophet (ﷺ) saw a page of the Torah in the hand of 'Umar bin Al-Khattaab, so he said,

أمتهوكون يا ابن الخطاب؟! لقد جئتكم بها بيضاء نقية، لو كان موسى حيا و اتبعتموه و تركتموني ضللتم

"Have you all become *Mutahawwikoon* [9] O Ibn Al-Khattaab?! Indeed I have brought it (guidance) to you all, white and clean. If Moosaa were alive and you all followed him and abandoned me, you would have gone astray."

---

[9] *Mutahawwik*: One who has fallen into something without proper consideration, or who is confused. See *An-Nihaayah* of Ibn Al-Atheer.

In another narration he said,

لو كان موسى حيا ما وسعه إلا اتباعي فقال عمر: رضيت بالله ربا وبالإسلام دينا وبمحمد نبيا

"If Moosaa were alive, he would have no choice but to follow me." 'Umar then said, "I am pleased with Allaah as a Lord, Islaam as a religion, and Muhammad as a Prophet." [10]

---

[10] This is clear in His statement, Magnificent and Exalted is He (the English meaning is),

"And whoever seeks a religion other than Islaam, it will never be accepted of him." *Aal 'Imraan (3):85*

And in His statement (the English meaning is):

"And let those who oppose the Messenger's (Muhammad (ﷺ)) commandment (i.e. his *Sunnah* -- legal ways, orders, acts of worship, statements, etc.) (among the sects) beware, lest some *Fitnah* (disbelief, trials, afflictions, earthquakes, killing, overpowering by a tyrant, etc.) befall them or a painful torment be inflicted on them." *An-Noor (24):63*

And in His statement (the English meaning is),

"And whatsoever the Messenger (Muhammad (ﷺ)) gives you, take it; and whatsoever he forbids you, abstain (from it)." *Al-Hashr (59):7*

Therefore, it is obligatory upon the entire *Ummah* to follow him (ﷺ). And if Moosaa, or 'Eesaa, or anyone besides them (from the Prophets) were alive, they would have no choice but to follow him, because he was sent to all the people. Allaah said (the English meaning is),

"Say (O Muhammad (ﷺ)): 'O mankind! Verily, I am sent to you all as the Messenger of Allaah.'" *Al-A'raaf (7):158*

Therefore, it is obligatory upon all of the *Ummah* -- men, women, Arabs, non-Arabs, humans and Jinns -- to follow him (ﷺ), and to submit to his Law according to what has come in the Noble Qur'aan and the purified *Sunnah*. They have no right to go outside of that.

What has been reported concerning leaving the call of Islaam

Allaah says,

﴿ هُوَ سَمَّىٰكُمُ ٱلْمُسْلِمِينَ مِن قَبْلُ وَفِي هَٰذَا ﴾

"It is He (Allaah) Who has named you Muslims both before and in this (the Qur'aan)." *Al-Hajj (22):78*

It is narrated from Al-Haarith Al-Ash'aree that the Prophet (ﷺ) said,

آمركم بخمس، الله أمرني بهن: السمع، والطاعة، والجها د، والهجرة، والجماعة، فإنه من فارق الجماعة قيد شبر فقد خلع ربقة الإسلام من عنقه إلا أن يراجع، ومن دعا بدعوى الجاهلية فإنه من جثي جهنم فقال رجل: يا رسول الله وإن صلى و صام قال: وإن صلى و صام فا دعوا بدعوى الله الذي سماكم المسلمين والمؤمنين عبا د الله

"I command you all with five things that Allaah has commanded me with: to listen (to those in authority), to obey (those in authority), to wage *Jihaad* (fighting in the Way of Allaah), to make *Hijrah* (migration to the lands of the Muslims), and adherence to the *Jamaa'ah* (the Muslim body or community). For whoever separates from the *Jamaa'ah* even a hand span, then he has removed the noose of Islaam from around his neck, unless he comes back. And whoever calls with the call of the days of ignorance (i.e. racism, tribalism, bigoted partisanship, etc.), then verily, he is from the dwellers of Hell." A man said, "O Messenger of Allaah! Even if he prays and fasts?" The Prophet replied, "Even if he prays and fasts. So call with the call of Allaah, Who named you Muslims, believers (*Mu'mineen*), and slaves of Allaah." (Ahmad and At-Tirmidhee. At-Tirmidhee said it is a good authentic *hadeeth*.) [11]

---

[11] And this is a warning against the call of pre-Islaamic ignorance (*Jaahiliyyah*), "O family of so-and-so, O family of so-and-so!" No. (Rather it should be) "O people of *At-Tawheed* (Islaamic monotheism, the worship of Allaah alone), O people of *Al-Eemaan* (faith)!" All of them are brothers. If war comes, they do not ascribe themselves to family lineages (saying), "O family of so-and-so, O family of Qahtaan, O Banee this and Banee that!" No. They are one thing. So the Muslims are a single thing (i.e. one body). They do not argue with the call of pre-Islaamic ignorance. For this reason, when the man said, "O Immigrants (*Muhaajiroon*)", and another man said, "O Helpers (*Ansaar*)", the Prophet (ﷺ) said, **"Is it with the call of pre-Islaamic ignorance (that you are calling with), while I am still amongst you?"** Therefore it is obligatory to use the call

It is narrated in the *Saheeh* that the Prophet (ﷺ) said,

من فارق الجماعة شبرا فميتته جاهلية

"Whoever separates from the *Jamaa'ah* (the Muslim body or community) a hand span, then his death is an ignorant death."

In another narration in the *Saheeh* he said,

أبدعوى الجاهلية وأنا بين أظهركم

"Is it with the call of pre-Islaamic ignorance (that you are calling with), while I am still amongst you?"

Abul-'Abbaas said, "Everything that goes outside of the call of Islaam and the Qur'aan, whether it is of lineage, land, nationality, school of thought (*Madhhab*), or path of mysticism (*Tareeqah*), then it is from the ascriptions of the days of pre-Islaamic ignorance (*Jaahiliyyah*).[12] When a man from the

---

of Islaam. "O brothers!" "O Muslims!" And so forth, when calling for support, and encouraging the people. One should encourage them to fight in the name of Islaam and in the name of *Eemaan* (faith).

[12] The intent here is that the calls that are other than the call of Islaam, such as saying, "O people of Makkah!", "O people of Taa'if!", "O people of Najd!", "O people of wherever", this is from the calls of pre-Islaamic ignorance. Rather, the person should say, "O believers!", "O brothers!", "O helpers of Allaah!", "O slaves of Allaah!", and so forth.

Immigrants (*Muhaajiroon*) and a man from the Helpers (*Ansaar*) disputed, and the Immigrant said, 'O Immigrants!' And the man from the *Ansaar* said, 'O Helpers!' The Prophet (ﷺ) said,

أبدعوى الجاهلية وأنا بين أظهركم؟

'Is it with the call of pre-Islaamic ignorance (that you are calling with), while I am still amongst you?' And he became extremely angry at this." [13]

---

[13] This is what is obligatory, and this is what will encourage them and move the hearts. So when meeting the enemy, one should encourage them (the Muslims) to meet their enemy and be patient by using the call of *Eemaan* (faith) and the call of Islaam. "O Muslims!", "O army of Allaah!", "O slaves of Allaah!", "O Muslims!", "O helpers of Allaah!" and so forth. He should encourage them like this and incite them (to fight) with the inclusive or encompassing Islaam (i.e. it includes everyone of the Muslims).

The obligation of entering Islaam entirely and abandoning everything other than it

Allaah says,

﴿ يَٰٓأَيُّهَا ٱلَّذِينَ ءَامَنُواْ ٱدۡخُلُواْ فِي ٱلسِّلۡمِ كَآفَّةٗ ﴾

"O you who believe! Enter perfectly in *As-Silm* (Islaam)." *Al-Baqarah (2):208*

Allaah also says,

﴿ أَلَمۡ تَرَ إِلَى ٱلَّذِينَ يَزۡعُمُونَ أَنَّهُمۡ ءَامَنُواْ بِمَآ أُنزِلَ إِلَيۡكَ

وَمَآ أُنزِلَ مِن قَبۡلِكَ يُرِيدُونَ أَن يَتَحَاكَمُوٓاْ إِلَى ٱلطَّٰغُوتِ

وَقَدۡ أُمِرُوٓاْ أَن يَكۡفُرُواْ بِهِۦ وَيُرِيدُ ٱلشَّيۡطَٰنُ أَن يُضِلَّهُمۡ

ضَلَٰلَۢا بَعِيدٗا ﴾

"Have you seen those (hypocrites) who claim that they believe in that which has been sent down to you (O Muhammad (ﷺ)), and that which was sent down before you (O Muhammad (ﷺ)), and they wish to go for judgement (in their disputes) to the *Taaghoot* (false judges, etc.) while they have been

ordered to reject them. But *Shaytaan* (Satan) wishes to lead them far astray." *An-Nisaa' (4):60*

And Allaah says,

﴿ إِنَّ ٱلَّذِينَ فَرَّقُواْ دِينَهُمْ وَكَانُواْ شِيَعًا لَّسْتَ مِنْهُمْ فِى شَىْءٍ ﴾

"Verily, those who divide their religion and break up into sects (all kinds of religious sects), you (O Muhammad (ﷺ)) have no concern in them in the least." *Al-An'aam (6):159* [14]

---

[14] This is what is obligatory. That the person must enter Islaam, all of it and not just some of it. Allaah said (the English meaning is),

"O you who believe! Enter perfectly in *As-Silm* (Islaam)." *Al-Baqarah (2):208*

Meaning, into Islaam. And He, the Most High, says (the English meaning is),

"Verily, those who divide their religion and break up into sects (all kinds of religious sects), you (O Muhammad (ﷺ)) have no concern in them in the least." *Al-An'aam (6):159*

And He, the Magnificent and Exalted, says (the English meaning is),

"Verily, those who disbelieve in Allaah and His Messengers and wish to make distinction between Allaah and His Messengers (by believing in Allaah and disbelieving in His Messengers) saying, 'We believe in some but reject others,' and wish to adopt a way in between. They are in truth disbelievers." *An-Nisaa' (4):150-151*

Thus, it is obligatory to enter into Islaam, all of it. Meaning, what is obligatory is that the Muslim adheres to all of Islaam -- the prayer (*As-Salaah*), obligatory

And Allaah says,

﴿ يَوْمَ تَبْيَضُّ وُجُوهٌ وَتَسْوَدُّ وُجُوهٌ ۚ فَأَمَّا ٱلَّذِينَ ٱسْوَدَّتْ وُجُوهُهُمْ أَكَفَرْتُم بَعْدَ إِيمَٰنِكُمْ فَذُوقُوا۟ ٱلْعَذَابَ بِمَا كُنتُمْ تَكْفُرُونَ ﴾

"On the Day when some faces will become white and some faces will become black; as for those whose faces will become black (to them it will be said): 'Did you reject faith after accepting it? Then taste the torment (in Hell) for rejecting faith.'" *Aal 'Imraan (3):106*

Ibn 'Abbaas said, "The faces of the people of the *Sunnah* and unity (*I'tilaaf*) will become white, and the faces of the people of innovations (*Bid'ah*) and differing (*Ikhtilaaf*) will become black."

'Abdullaah bin 'Umar narrated that the Messenger of Allaah (ﷺ) said,

---

charity (*Az-Zakaah*), fasting (*As-Siyaam*), pilgrimage to Makkah (*Al-Hajj*), and *Jihaad*. He does not say, "I will only pray but I will not give *Zakaah*." Or, "I will give *Zakaah* but I won't fast." No. It is obligatory upon the person to adhere to all of Islaam.

ليأتين على أمتي ما أتي على بني إسرائيل حذو النعل بالنعل، حتى إن كان منهم من أتى أمه علانية كان في أمتي من يصنع ذلك، وأن بني إسرائيل افترقت على اثنتين و سبعين ملة

"Indeed there will come upon my *Ummah* (followers) that which came upon the Children of Israel, sandal by sandal (i.e. step by step). Even if there is among them a man who has sexual intercourse with his own mother openly, there will be someone from my followers who will do that as well. And indeed the Children of Israel broke up into seventy-two sects."

The Prophet (ﷺ) concluded his statement by saying,

وتفترق هذه الأمة على ثلاث و سبعين فرقة كلهم في النار إلا ملة واحدة - قالوا: من هي يا رسول الله ؟ قال: ما أنا عليه وأ صحابي

"This *Ummah* (nation of Muslims) will divide into seventy-three sects. All of them will be in the Hellfire except one religion (sect)." They (the Companions) said, "Who are they (the saved sect), O Messenger of Allaah?!" He replied, "(They are upon) what I and my Companions (the *Sahaabah*) are upon."

The believer who hopes in the meeting with Allaah should pay attention to the speech of the truthful one (*As-Saadiq*), the one who was trusted in what he was sent with (*Al-Masdooq*), [15] particularly in this matter.

ما أنا عليه وأصحابي

"What I and my companions (the *Sahaabah*) are upon."

Oh what an admonition this is if it falls upon hearts that are alive. This *hadeeth* was reported by At-Tirmidhee, and he also reported it from Abu Hurairah and he declared it authentic. However, the version he reported from Abu Hurairah does not contain the mentioning of the Hellfire. It has also been narrated in a *hadeeth* of Mu'aawiyyah that was collected by Ahmad and Abu Daawood and it contains the following wording:

---

[15] Meaning, the person must adhere to the truth and stand firm upon what the Companions, and their successors traversed upon in goodness. And the person must beware of the statements of the people of innovations, separation and differing. **"Seventy two sects, all of them are in the fire."** These sects include those who may be disbelievers, innovators or sinful transgressors. However, the people of the *Sunnah* and the *Jamaa'ah*, they are those who traverse upon the path of the Companions, and they stand firm upon the *Deen*. So these people, they will have Paradise and honor. In reference to the rest of the sects, they have disbelievers among them, innovators among them, and among them there are those who oppose the Law of Islaam and do not adhere to the truth.

إنه سيخرج من أمتي قوم تتجارى بهم تلك الأهواء كما يتجارى الكلب بصاحبه، فلا يبقى منه عرق ولا مفصل إلا دخله

"Indeed there shall appear a group of people from my *Ummah* (followers) that will be overcome by these desires (deviations) just as a dog is overcome by its rabies. There does not remain any vein or joint in him except that it enters it."

And it has already been mentioned previously that the Prophet (ﷺ) said,

ومبتغ في الإسلام سنة الجاهلية

"...and the one who seeks to introduce the way (*sunnah*) of the days of pre-Islaamic ignorance (*Jaahiliyyah*)[16] into Islaam." [17]

---

[16] Meaning, it is obligatory for the Muslims to beware of innovating in the *Deen*. They must beware of the ways of pre-Islaamic ignorance. Rather, it is obligatory upon them to adhere to the Islaam that *Al-Mustafaa* (the chosen one) (ﷺ) came with, and that they work together in this and advise each other with this. So they should carry out what Allaah legislated and avoid whatever Allaah forbade. They must beware of the innovations and the sins. Likewise, it is obligatory upon the people of Islaam to stand firm and cooperate upon righteousness and piety, as Allaah, the Most High, said (the English meaning is),

"Help you one another in *Al-Birr* and *At-Taqwa* (virtue, righteousness and piety)." *Al-Maa'idah (5):2*

And He said (the English meaning is),

> **"By the time. Verily! Man is in loss. Except those who believe and do righteous good deeds, and recommend one another to the truth and recommend one another to patience."** *Al-'Asr (103):1-3*

However, concerning the matter of them dividing, such that one says, "I will take this", and another says, "I will take that", then this is not permissible. This is the *Deen* of pre-Islaamic ignorance. We ask Allaah for safety and well-being (from that).

[17] And its chains of narration together reach the level of being *Hasan* (good).

What has been reported concerning innovation being worse than the major sins [18]

---

[18] This means that innovation is greater than the major sins because it is to find deficiency in Islaam, and it introduces things into Islaam and it is an implicit way of accusing Islaam of being deficient.

This is why the person innovates and adds things (i.e. because he feels Islaam is not enough as it is). In reference to the sins, then it is following the desires and obeying the devil (*Ash-Shaytaan*), so it is lighter than innovation, and the one who commits sins may repent, and rush to do good and adhere to the truth. But the person of innovation, he thinks that he is correct and that he is striving upon goodness.

Therefore, he continues with the innovation. We seek refuge with Allaah from this. He thinks the *Deen* is deficient, so he needs his innovation. For this reason, the matter of innovation is more serious and dangerous than acts of disobedience (i.e. sins). Allaah, the Most High, said regarding the people of sins (the English meaning is),

"But He forgives except that (anything else) to whom He pleases." *An-Nisaa' (4):48*

So the people who commit sinful acts of disobedience are left to the will of Allaah, and the people of innovations, their sin is tremendous and the danger of their affair is severe because their innovation means that Islaam is deficient and that it needs this innovation. The person of this innovation thinks that he is right, and he persists in it, and remains upon it, and he argues in defense of it. We ask Allaah for safety and well-being (from this).

Allaah says,

﴿ إِنَّ ٱللَّهَ لَا يَغۡفِرُ أَن يُشۡرَكَ بِهِۦ وَيَغۡفِرُ مَا دُونَ ذَٰلِكَ لِمَن يَشَآءُ ﴾

"Verily, Allaah forgives not that partners should be set up with him in worship, but He forgives except that (anything else) to whom He pleases." *An-Nisaa' (4):48* [19]

Allaah also says,

﴿ لِيَحۡمِلُوٓاْ أَوۡزَارَهُمۡ كَامِلَةً يَوۡمَ ٱلۡقِيَٰمَةِ ۙ وَمِنۡ أَوۡزَارِ ٱلَّذِينَ يُضِلُّونَهُم بِغَيۡرِ عِلۡمٍ ۗ أَلَا سَآءَ مَا يَزِرُونَ ﴾

"That they may bear their own burdens in full on the Day of Resurrection, and also of the burdens of

---

[19] Here the author has mentioned this verse due to the relationship between *Shirk* and *Bid'ah* (innovating in the religion) as can be seen in Allaah's statement (the English meaning is),

"Or have they partners with Allaah (false gods), who have instituted for them a religion which Allaah has not allowed?" *Ash-Shooraa (42):21*

Hence, the innovator is not necessarily a polytheist (*Mushrik*), but he is behaving with a characteristic of the polytheists in his legislating into religious acts that which Allaah has not sanctioned.

those whom they misled without knowledge. Evil indeed is that which they shall bear!" *An-Nahl (16):25* [20]

In the *Saheeh* it is narrated that the Prophet (ﷺ) said about the *Khawaarij,* [21]

أينما لقيتموهم فاقتلوهم، لئن لقيتهم لأقتلنهم قتل عا د

---

[20] The statement of Allaah, the Most High (the English meaning is),

"And also of the burdens of those whom they misled..." *An-Nahl (16):25*

This means that upon him is a burden (of guilt) similar to the burdens of those who followed him in his innovation. We ask Allaah for safety and well-being (from this).

[21] *Khawaarij* (Kharijites): The first sect that broke away from mainstream Islaam by choosing their own interpretation of religious texts over that of the Prophet's Companions. They called everyone who committed a major sin (*kabeerah*) a disbeliever (*kaafir*) and held it to be incumbent upon every Muslim to fight against him. They waged war against the Prophet's companions after the Prophet's death and were eventually defeated by an army lead by 'Alee bin Abee Taalib at the Battle of An-Nahrawaan. However, their ideas still remained with some people and they developed other deviant theological and political views that always set them at war with the rest of the Muslim *Ummah*. Most of their sub-sects have now vanished; however some remnants of them are still found in South-Eastern parts of the Arabian Peninsula. Their ideas also have been revived in the teachings of Hasan Al-Banna, Sayyid Qutub and those groups that embraced their teachings, like *Al-Ikhwaan ul-Muslimeen* (the Muslim Brotherhood).

"Wherever you find them, then kill them, for indeed if I were to meet them, I would certainly kill them like the killing of (the people of) 'Aad." [22]

[22] **"Indeed if I were to meet them, I would certainly kill them like the killing of (the people of) 'Aad."** This is due to the tremendous nature of their innovation, because they caused the people to be confused (about the truth). So diligent they were in their recitation (of the Qur'aan) and their prayers (*As-Salaah*) that the Prophet (ﷺ) said, **"One of you (the Companions) would consider his prayer like nothing compared to their prayer, and his recitation like nothing compared to their recitation."** Then they turned against the Muslims (i.e. the Companions) and killed them. This was due to their wicked boldness. So they fought against 'Alee (bin Abee Taalib) and they killed 'Umar bin Khaarijah [***Editor's Note:*** *Perhaps this is a misprint in the Arabic print of the book that was used for the translation as it is well-known in the history books that the Khawaarij killed Khaarijah bin Hudhaafah. As for 'Umar bin Khaarijah, then I have not seen his name in the books of history, and Allaah knows best*], and they killed a large number of people. All of this was due to their innovation and their misguidance, until Allaah aided 'Alee against them and he killed them. So the *Khawaarij*, their evil is great because they think that they are right in their murdering the sinful rulers and people other than the rulers as well. This is due to their ignorance and their misguidance. For this reason, the Prophet (ﷺ) said about them, **"Wherever you find them, then kill them, for verily in killing them there is a reward for whoever kills them."** And he said, **"If I were to meet them, I would certainly kill them like the killing of 'Aad."**

Someone interjected and asked the Shaykh (*Rahimahullaah*), "Does innovation enter into that which is left to the will of Allaah if it is not an innovation that makes one a disbeliever?"

So the Eminent Shaykh answered by saying, "It is not considered among the regular sins, because it is something that there is a threat of Hellfire for it, and refuge is sought with Allaah. Unless the person repents, and we ask Allaah for safety and well-being. However, if it is less than *Shirk*, it is hoped for its

It is also reported in the *Saheeh* that he forbade killing the tyrannical leaders as long as they pray (*As-Salaah*).[23]

Jareer narrated from 'Abdullaah that a man gave some charity, then the people began giving charity after him. Then the Messenger of Allaah (ﷺ) said,

من سن في الإسلام سنة حسنة فله أجرها وأجر من عمل
بها من بعده من غير أن ينقص من أجورهم شيء، ومن

---

practitioner (that he may be saved), because it is included in the meaning of the meanings of disobedience (i.e. sins). However, it is not included in Allaah's statement (the English meaning is),

"But He forgives except that (anything else) to whom He pleases." *An-Nisaa' (4):48*

In general it is not included in this (i.e. these sins). However if the innovator's innovation is less than *Shirk*, then it has the ruling of the acts of disobedience from a certain aspect, in that the person will not remain in the Hellfire forever if he enters the Fire.

[23] Meaning the rulers, even if they are tyranical and oppressive, as long as they adhere to Islaam, it is not permissible to make *Jihaad* (to fight) against them. However, they are to be advised. But if they commit clear disbelief, it is obligatory to wage *Jihaad* against them for whoever is able, if there is the strength available to do so. I say: this means they should strive to remove them as long as that does not involve bringing harm to the Muslims (i.e. the common masses).

سن في الإسلام سنة سيئة كان عليه وزرها و وزر من عمل بها من غير أن ينقص من أوزارهم شيء

"Whoever starts a good *Sunnah* in Islaam, then he will have its reward, and the reward of whoever acts according to it after him without decreasing anything from their rewards in the least. And whoever starts an evil *Sunnah* (way) in Islaam, then upon him is its burden (of sin), and the burden of whoever acts according to it after him without decreasing anything from their burdens in the least." (Muslim) [24]

---

[24] This is its meaning: he revives it (this *Sunnah*) and he manifests it. It does not mean that it is permissible to innovate. Rather, it only means the revival of the *Sunnah* and making it manifest, because he (ﷺ) saw some people who were poor, and when he saw their poverty he gave a sermon to the people, and encouraged them to give charity, urging them to do so. He (the narrator) said, **"Each man gave from his gold and silver coins, and his garments, and his *Saa'* of wheat, and his *Saa'* of dried dates until the Prophet (ﷺ) said, 'Even if it is a half of a dried date.'"**

So the narrator went on to say, "So a man came from among the *Ansaar* with a container that his hands could barely hold, and actually he was not able to hold it. Then the people followed him until I saw two small hills, one of food and one of clothing. This continued until I saw the face of the Messenger of Allaah (ﷺ) become bright as if he were overcome with delight. So the Messenger of Allaah (ﷺ) said, **'Whoever starts a good *Sunnah* in Islaam, then he will have its reward, and the reward of whoever acts according to it after him without decreasing anything from their rewards in the least. And whoever starts an evil *Sunnah* (way) in Islaam, then upon him is its burden (of sin), and the burden of whoever acts according to it after him without decreasing anything from their burdens in the least.'"**

This *hadeeth* has also been recorded from Abu Hurairah with the wording,

من دعا إلى هدى - ثم قال - من دعا إلى ضلالة

"Whoever calls to guidance..." then he said, "Whoever calls to misguidance."

The Shaykh was asked (*Rahimahullaah*) the following question: The person who praises the people of innovation and speaks highly of them, is he considered to be with them? The eminent Shaykh responded by saying, "Yes, there is no doubt that the one who praises them and commends them, then he is a caller to them. He is considered one of their callers. We ask Allaah for safety and well-being from this."

What has been narrated concerning the practitioner of innovation being prevented from repentance [25]

[25] The intent of this chapter is to clarify the danger of innovation (*Al-Bid'ah*) and that from the dangers of innovation is that the person who practices it will not be guided (by Allaah) to making repentance. He will think that he is correct and he will continue in falsehood. This is from the dangers of it (innovation) and its trials. Thus, it is obligatory to beware of innovations because they are a tremendous evil. This is just as the Messenger of Allaah (ﷺ) mentioned in the authentic *hadeeth*, **"Whoever does a deed that is not from our matter (i.e. our *Deen*, our *Sharee'ah*), then it is rejected."** And he (ﷺ) said, **"Every innovation is a misguidance."** There is no power or strength except with Allaah.

The Shaykh (*Rahimahullaah*) was asked about the authenticity of the *hadeeth*, **"Verily Allaah does not accept the *Tawbah* (repentance) of every practitioner of innovation."**

The Eminent Shaykh answered by saying, "The *hadeeth* needs some attention and investigation into its chain of narration. However, this is something feared for them. This is because the usual case with them is that they think good of their opinions and they remain upon them. We ask Allaah for safety and well-being. Yet, there are many people from the people of innovation who repent and Allaah accepts their repentance. And if this *hadeeth* is authentic, then it is from the matter of threatening and warning. We ask Allaah for safety and well-being. This is similar to what the Prophet (ﷺ) said regarding Al-Madeenah. **"Whoever introduces any innovation in it (i.e. the city of Madeenah), or he gives shelter to an innovator, then upon him is the curse of Allaah, the Angels and all of the people. Allaah will not accept from him any optional deed nor any obligatory deed on the Day of Resurrection."** This is from the matter of threatening. Otherwise, whoever repents, Allaah accepts his repentance.

This has been reported from Anas and it is among the *Mursal* [26] narrations of Al-Hasan. [27]

Then the Shaykh responded in one of the lessons about this *hadeeth* and its meaning by saying, "And this is the truth, that Allaah places a veil between repentance and the practitioner of innovation. This means that he thinks his innovation is good and he thinks he is right. For this reason, you usually find that he dies while still being upon that innovation, and Allaah's refuge is sought. This is because he thinks that he is right, contrary to the person of sinful disobedience, who knows that he is disobedient, and a sinner, and that he is doing wrong. So such a person may repent and Allaah will accept his repentance. However, the practitioner of innovation is upon a dangerous matter because he thinks his innovation is good and he follows his desires. So for this reason he is upon something dangerous, and he is blocked from repentance due to his thinking good of his innovation, and his thinking he is upon guidance, and his belief that he is upon the truth. However, if Allaah guides him and he sees right and repents, then Allaah will accept his repentance. And all sins, if the slave of Allaah repents from them, Allaah will accept his repentance, even if it is *Shirk*, which is a greater sin than innovation. So even disbelief in Allaah, if the slave of Allaah repents from that, then Allaah will accept his repentance. And the disbelievers from the Quraysh and others besides them, when they repented, Allaah accepted their repentance. Likewise the magicians of Fir'awn (Pharoah), when they repented, Allaah accepted their repentance. So similarly, the practitioner of innovation, if Allaah blesses him to see right, and he repents from that innovation, Allaah accepts his repentance. So this (*hadeeth*) is from the matter of threatening. It is similar to the authentic *hadeeth*, **"Whoever introduces any innovation in it (i.e. the city of Al-Madeenah), or he gives shelter to an innovator, then upon him is the curse of Allaah, the Angels and all of the people. Allaah will not accept from him any optional deed nor any obligatory deed on the Day of Resurrection."** Therefore, it is from the matter of threatening.

[26] *Mursal*: This is a term used to classify a *hadeeth* that has been narrated from a successor (in this case, Al-Hasan Al-Basree) when he reports directly from the

Ibn Wadhdhaah narrated from Ayyoob that he said, "There was a man among us who held an opinion (that was deviant), but then he abandoned it. Then I went to Muhammad bin Seereen and I said, 'Do you feel that so-and-so has abandoned his view?' He replied, 'Look at what he has changed to now.' Verily the end of the *hadeeth* (about the *Khawaarij*) is more severe against them than the beginning of it:

يمرقون من الإسلام كما يمرق السهم من الرمية ثم لا يعودون إليه

'They will leave out of Islaam just as the arrow leaves out of the bow, then they will not return to it.'"

Ahmad bin Hanbal was asked about the meaning of this and he said, "They will not be guided to repentance."

Prophet without mentioning who narrated the *hadeeth* to him. In essence such *ahadeeth* are actually weak, but in this case, this narration has been confirmed to be statement of the Prophet by way of Anas bin Maalik.

[27] The author is referring to the *hadeeth* which states that the Prophet said, **"Verily, Allaah veils (*hajaba*) -- or he said keeps back (*hajaza*) -- the (acceptance) of repentance from every practitioner of innovation until he leaves his innovation."** This *hadeeth* was recorded by Ibn Abee 'Aasim in *As-Sunnah* and At-Tabarani. Shaykh Al-Albaanee graded it *Saheeh* (authentic) in his checking of *Kitaab us-Sunnah*, no. 37.

The statement of Allaah: "O people of the Scripture (Jews and Christians)! Why do you dispute about Ibraaheem (Abraham)?"

Allaah says,

﴿ يَٰٓأَهۡلَ ٱلۡكِتَٰبِ لِمَ تُحَآجُّونَ فِيٓ إِبۡرَٰهِيمَ وَمَآ أُنزِلَتِ ٱلتَّوۡرَىٰةُ وَٱلۡإِنجِيلُ إِلَّا مِنۢ بَعۡدِهِۦٓۚ أَفَلَا تَعۡقِلُونَ ٦٥ هَٰٓأَنتُمۡ هَٰٓؤُلَآءِ حَٰجَجۡتُمۡ فِيمَا لَكُم بِهِۦ عِلۡمٞ فَلِمَ تُحَآجُّونَ فِيمَا لَيۡسَ لَكُم بِهِۦ عِلۡمٞۚ وَٱللَّهُ يَعۡلَمُ وَأَنتُمۡ لَا تَعۡلَمُونَ ٦٦ مَا كَانَ إِبۡرَٰهِيمُ يَهُودِيّٗا وَلَا نَصۡرَانِيّٗا وَلَٰكِن كَانَ حَنِيفٗا مُّسۡلِمٗا وَمَا كَانَ مِنَ ٱلۡمُشۡرِكِينَ ﴾

"O people of the Scripture (Jews and Christians)! Why do you dispute about Ibraaheem (Abraham), while the Torah and the Injeel (Gospel) were not revealed until after him? Have you then no sense? Verily, you are those who have disputed about that of which you have knowledge. Why do you then dispute concerning that of which you have no knowledge? It is Allaah Who knows, and you

know not. Ibraaheem (Abraham) was neither a Jew nor a Christian, but he was a true Muslim, *Haneef* (upright upon Islaamic Monotheism - worshipping Allaah Alone) and he was not of *Al-Mushrikeen* (those who worship others besides Allaah)." *Aal 'Imraan (3):65-67*

Allaah also says,

﴿وَمَن يَرْغَبُ عَن مِّلَّةِ إِبْرَاهِيمَ إِلَّا مَن سَفِهَ نَفْسَهُۥ ۚ وَلَقَدِ ٱصْطَفَيْنَٰهُ فِى ٱلدُّنْيَا ۖ وَإِنَّهُۥ فِى ٱلْءَاخِرَةِ لَمِنَ ٱلصَّٰلِحِينَ﴾

"And who turns away from the religion of Ibraaheem (Abraham) except him who befools himself? Truly, We chose him in this world and verily, in the Hereafter he will be among the righteous." *Al-Baqarah (2):130*

Concerning this, there is the *hadeeth* of the *Khawaarij* which has preceded.

Also, it is narrated that he (the Prophet (ﷺ)) said,

آل أبي فلان ليسوا لي بأولياء إنما أوليائي المتقون

"The family of Abu so-and-so are not my *Awliyaa'* (supporters, protectors). My *Awliyaa'* are only the *Muttaqoon* (righteous, pious, God-fearing people)."

Anas narrated that it was mentioned to the Messenger of Allaah (ﷺ) that one of the Companions had said, "I will not eat meat." Another one said, "I will stand all night in prayer and not sleep." Another one said, "I will not marry women." Another one said, "I will fast and not break my fast." So the Prophet (ﷺ) said,

لكنني أقوم وأنام وأ صوم وأفطر وأتزوج النساء وآكل

اللحم فمن رغب عن سنتي فليس مني

"But I stand at night for prayer, and I sleep, and I fast, and I break my fast, and I marry women, and I eat meat. So whoever turns away from my *Sunnah*, then he is not of me." [28]

So take note! When some of the Companions wanted to devote themselves to worship, this harsh

---

[28] This contains a warning against overburdening oneself and extremism, and that it is obligatory upon the believer to beware of that. So he should fast, and pray, and perform optional prayers at night, and sleep, and leave off fasting and eat meat. He should sleep on a mattress and not overburden himself. For this reason the Prophet (ﷺ) said, **"But I stand at night for prayer, and I sleep, and I fast, and I break my fast, and I marry women, and I eat meat. So whoever turns away from my *Sunnah*, then he is not of me."** So Allaah legislated for His slaves that which will not be too difficult for them, and that which will not be hard on them. So it is not permissible to go to extremes and overburden oneself. And in the *Sunnah* of the Messenger (ﷺ) there is that which is sufficient, for he is the most virtuous of mankind, and the best of all the people (ﷺ).

statement was said concerning them, and their deeds were called "turning away from the *Sunnah*." So what do you think about innovations other than these? And what do you think about people who are not Companions (of the Prophet)?

The statement of Allaah: "So set you (O Muhammad) your face towards the religion (Islaam) being Haneef (worshipping none but Allaah Alone)."

Allaah says,

﴿ فَأَقِمْ وَجْهَكَ لِلدِّينِ حَنِيفًا ۚ فِطْرَتَ ٱللَّهِ ٱلَّتِى فَطَرَ ٱلنَّاسَ عَلَيْهَا ۚ لَا تَبْدِيلَ لِخَلْقِ ٱللَّهِ ۚ ذَٰلِكَ ٱلدِّينُ ٱلْقَيِّمُ وَلَٰكِنَّ أَكْثَرَ ٱلنَّاسِ لَا يَعْلَمُونَ ﴾

"So set you (O Muhammad (ﷺ)) your face towards the religion (Islaam) being *Haneef* (worshipping none but Allaah Alone). Allaah's *Fitrah* (Islaamic Monotheism) with which He has created mankind. Let there be no change in *Khalq-illaah* (i.e. Allaah's religion); that is the straight religion, but most of mankind know not." *Ar-Room (30):30*

Allaah also says,

﴿ وَوَصَّىٰ بِهَآ إِبْرَٰهِـۧمُ بَنِيهِ وَيَعْقُوبُ يَـٰبَنِىَّ إِنَّ ٱللَّهَ ٱصْطَفَىٰ لَكُمُ ٱلدِّينَ فَلَا تَمُوتُنَّ إِلَّا وَأَنتُم مُّسْلِمُونَ ﴾

"And this (submission to Allaah, Islaam) was enjoined by Ibraaheem (Abraham) upon his sons and by Ya'qoob (Jacob) (saying), 'O my sons! Allaah has chosen for you the (true) religion, then do not die except as Muslims.'" *Al-Baqarah (2):132*

Allaah also says,

﴿ ثُمَّ أَوْحَيْنَآ إِلَيْكَ أَنِ ٱتَّبِعْ مِلَّةَ إِبْرَٰهِيمَ حَنِيفًا ۖ وَمَا كَانَ مِنَ ٱلْمُشْرِكِينَ ﴾

"Then, We have sent the revelation to you (O Muhammad (ﷺ)) (saying): 'Follow the religion of Ibraaheem (Abraham) being *Haneef* (worshipping none but Allaah Alone),' and he (Ibraaheem) was not of the *Mushrikeen* (polytheists, idolaters, disbelievers)." *An-Nahl (16):123*

Ibn Mas'ood narrated that the Messenger of Allaah said,

إن لكل نبي ولاة من النبيين وأنا وليي منهم أبي إبراهيم وخليل ربي

"Verily, every Prophet had supporters from the Prophets, and regarding me, my supporter from among them is my father, Ibraaheem, and (he is) the *Khaleel* (intimate friend) of my Lord." Then he recited,

﴿ إِنَّ أَوْلَى ٱلنَّاسِ بِإِبْرَٰهِيمَ لَلَّذِينَ ٱتَّبَعُوهُ وَهَٰذَا ٱلنَّبِيُّ وَٱلَّذِينَ ءَامَنُوا۟ ۗ وَٱللَّهُ وَلِيُّ ٱلْمُؤْمِنِينَ ﴾

"Verily, among mankind who have the best claim to Ibraaheem (Abraham) are those who followed him, and this Prophet (Muhammad) and those who have believed (Muslims). And Allaah is the *Walee* (Protector and Helper) of the believers."
(*Aal 'Imraan (3):68)*" (At-Tirmidhee)

Abu Hurairah narrated that the Messenger of Allaah said,

إن الله لا ينظر إلى أجسامكم ولا إلى أموالكم ولكن ينظر إلى قلوبكم وأعمالكم

"Verily, Allaah does not look at your bodies or your wealth. Rather, He looks at your hearts and your deeds." [29]

---

[29] This *hadeeth* was reported by Muslim. It is his (ﷺ) statement, **"Verily, Allaah does not look at your bodies, or your wealth. Rather, he looks at your hearts and your deeds."** So the hearts are the place that Allaah looks at, and

It is narrated in the *Saheehayn* (two authentic narrations) from Ibn Mas'ood that the Messenger of Allaah (ﷺ) said,

أنا فرطكم على الحوض وليرفعن إلي رجال من أمتي حتى إذا أهويت لأناولهم احجبوا دوني فأقول: أي رب أصحابي فيقال إنك لا تدري ما أحدثوا بعدك

"I will precede you all to the *Hawdh* (his pond or basin in the Hereafter), and some men will be brought to me from my *Ummah*. But when I try to reach out to them (to shake their hands) they will be prevented from coming near me. So I will say, 'O my

---

your deeds. In reference to the physical appearances and the wealth, they have no value if they are not used in the obedience of Allaah. However, the place that is looked at is the hearts. If the hearts stand firm upon the love of Allaah, and sincerity to Him, and fear of Him, and hope in Him, and the deeds are righteous, and they are done solely for Allaah, and they are in accordance with the *Sunnah*, this is that which will benefit the person. A righteous heart and righteous deeds.

The Shaykh was asked (*Rahimahullaah*) about the Prophet's (ﷺ) statement, **"Verily Allaah does not look..."**

So he responded by saying, "This means those things do not have any value. The intent behind negating the looking at them is that they have no value. This is like his saying, **"He will not look at them, nor will He purify them."** This is due to His anger with them, and there is nothing that is hidden from Him in the least. He sees everything, Magnificent and Exalted is He. However, the intent is the look of pleasure, and the look of love."

Lord! My *Ashaab* (companions, followers)!' Then it will be said, 'Verily, you do not know what they innovated after you.'" [30]

---

[30] And in another wording of it, **"Verily they have not ceased being apostates turning their backs since I left them."** And for this reason they will be prevented from the pond, because they apostated, and those who apostated in the time of Abu Bakr, they will be prevented from the pond. In reference to those who died upon their faith (i.e.. Islaam), then they will be allowed to come to the pond.

The Shaykh was asked (*Rahimahullaah*) about the Prophet's (ﷺ) statement in the *hadeeth*, **"O my Lord! My companions!"**

So he responded by saying, "His Companions who were with him and then some of the people (from among them) apostated after they had entered Islaam in his time (ﷺ), and some people apostated in the time of As-Siddeeq (Abu Bakr), and As-Siddeeq and the Companions fought them."

The Shaykh was asked (*Rahimahullaah*) about the rebellious sinner, wouldn't he be allowed to come to the pond as well?

So the Shaykh answered saying, "The apparent meaning of the *hadeeth* includes him, because he is not an apostate. However, his situation is dangerous. It has come in some of the narrations that he is under threat as well, so he must beware. The threat (here) is only regarding those who apostate from Islaam, that they will continue in their apostasy, turning on their heels from the time that he (ﷺ) left them. However, in reference to the disobedient sinner, then he is not an apostate. He is deficient in faith, weak in faith, so it is feared for him, thus he must beware.

The Shaykh was asked (*Rahimahullaah*) about the people of innovation, are they from among those who will be pushed away from the basin?

So he answered saying, "Concerning the people of innovation, there is some distinction between them. Among them there are those who are disbelievers, and among them there are Muslims. In reference to the innovator who is a disbeliever, then he will not be allowed to come (to the pond). We ask Allaah for safety and well-being (from this)."

The Shaykh was asked (*Rahimahullaah*) about the *Raafidhah* (i.e. Shiites), are they from among the seventy-two (deviant) sects?

So he answered by saying, "They are included in them. However, among them there are disbelievers, and among them there are Muslims. So the *Raafidhah* who are worshippers of other than Allaah, then they are disbelievers. And the *Raafidhah* who prefer 'Alee over 'Uthmaan, or over As-Siddeeq (Abu Bakr), then these people are not disbelievers, however they are innovators. However, whoever supplicates to 'Alee, or to a member of the Prophet's family (i.e. *Ahlul-Bayt*) and they exaggerate concerning them, then verily such people are disbelievers. Or whoever says, "Verily the Prophethood really should have been for 'Alee, but Jibraa'eel was treacherous (by coming to Muhammad instead)," then this person is a disbeliever and an apostate. We ask Allaah for safety and well-being (from this).

And the seventy-two sects, among them are disbelievers, and among them there are disobedient sinners. Among them there are misguided innovators, and innovators who are not disbelievers. However, all of them have come together in the matter of answering the call of the Prophet (ﷺ). So they are from the *Ummah* of *Al-Ijaabah* (answering the call). In reference to the *Ummah* of *Ad-Da'wah* (those who are to be called), then they are numerous. The Jews and the Christians are from the *Ummah* of *Ad-Da'wah*, and they are worthless. They are of the people of the Hellfire. However, these seventy-three sects, they are those who have answered the call (of Islaam) and they claim that they are from the followers of the Prophet (ﷺ). They claim that they have answered his call. The saved one from amongst them, the safe one is the Saved Sect (*Al-Firqatun-Naajiyyah*). They are those who follow the Prophet (ﷺ) and traverse upon his path. In reference to the seventy-two sects, then among them there is the deviant person, and among them there is the disbeliever, and among them there is the disobedient sinner, and among them there is the misguided innovator.

They are in various degrees and levels, and they are threatened with the Hellfire, all of them. We ask Allaah for safety and well-being (from this)."

The Shaykh was asked (*Rahimahullaah*), "Is there a difference between the one who knows and the one who is ignorant?"

So he answered by saying, "The matters differ. In some matters the ignorant person is excused and in some matters the ignorant person is not excused."

The Shaykh was asked (*Rahimahullaah*) about the *Raafidhah* and are they excused due to ignorance?

So he answered, "Whoever supplicates to other than Allaah, and he seeks help from other than Allaah (i.e. in matters that only Allaah controls), then he is a disbeliever absolutely. This is because they are living among Muslims, and the Qur'aan has reached them, and the *Sunnah* has reached them. Allaah made the Qur'aan as a warner and conveyor of a message. Allaah said (the English meaning is),

"This (Qur'aan) is a Message for mankind." *Ibraaheem (14):52*

And He said (the English meaning is),

"This Qur'aan has been revealed to me that I may therewith warn you and whomsoever it may reach." *Al-An'aam (6):19*

So whoever disbelieves while he is presently living among the Muslims, and he seeks help from other than Allaah (in matters that only Allaah can control), or he worships Al-Badawee or other than him, regardless of whether he is from the *Raafidhah* or not, then he has the ruling of *Kufr* (disbelief). We ask Allaah for safety and well-being."

The Shaykh (*Rahimahullaah*) was asked about some people who say, "Verily the followers of the *Al-Ibaadhiyyah* (in Oman), and the followers of *Az-Zaydiyyah* (in Yemen) are better than many of those who ascribe themselves to the four

It is also narrated in the two *Saheehs* on the authority of Abu Hurairah that Messenger of Allaah (ﷺ) said,

و د دت أنا قد رأينا إخواننا قالوا: أولسنا إخوانك يا ر سول الله ؟ قال: أنتم أ صحابي، وإخواني هم الذين لم يأتوا بعد قالوا: فكيف تعرف من لم يأت بعد من أمتك؟ قال: أرأيتم لو أن رجلاً له خيل غر محجلة بين ظهري خيل دهم بهم ألا يعرف خيله؟ قالوا: بلى قال: فإنهم يأتون غر محجلين من الوضوء وأنا فرطهم على الحوض، ألا ليذا دن رجال يوم القيامة عن حوضي كما يذا د البعير الضال أنا ديهم ألا هلم فيقال: إنهم قد بدلوا بعدك فأقول: سحقا سحقا

Madhhabs."

So he answered by saying, "The consideration is not based on the four *Madhhabs*. Rather, the consideration should be regarding the *'Aqeedah* (beliefs). The consideration should be based on Allaah said, His Messenger said. In reference to the four *Madhhabs*, then among their followers are deviant people, and among their followers are Muslims. However, what is important is to adhere to the Book of Allaah and the *Sunnah* of His Messenger (ﷺ), and to traverse upon the *Manhaj* (methodology) of the Companions, and those who followed the Companions of the Prophet (ﷺ) in the worship of Allaah alone, and standing firm upon His religion, and leaving off innovations. These people, they are the People of the *Sunnah* and the *Jamaa'ah* (*Ahlus-Sunnah wal-Jamaa'ah*)."

"I would love it if we could see our brothers." They (the Companions) said, "Are we not your brothers, O Messenger of Allaah?" He replied, "You all are my Companions. My brothers are those who have not come yet." They said, "How will you know those who have not come yet from your *Ummah*?" He replied, "If there is a man who has horses with distinctive white patches on their foreheads and legs, and his horses are among horses that are solid black, don't you think he would know his horses?" They replied, "Of course." Then he said, "Well verily, they (my brothers) will come with distinct white markings on their foreheads and limbs from the ablution (*Wudoo'*), and I will precede them to the pond (*Al-Hawdh*). And indeed there will be men who will be driven away from my pond on the Day of Resurrection just as the stray camel is driven away. I will call out to them saying, 'Come on!' But it will be said, 'Verily, they changed (the religion) after you.' So I will say (to them), 'Get away, get away!'" [31]

Al-Bukhaaree narrated a *hadeeth* in which the Prophet said,

---

[31] Allaah is the Greatest! Allaah is the Greatest! This means, be far away, be far away, for whoever changed things after me. And there is no power or strength except with Allaah. And this is the sign of his *Ummah*, *Ghurran Muhajjaleen* due to the traces of the *Wudoo'* of the *Ummah* of Muhammad, those who answered his call (ﷺ).

بينما أنا قائم إذا زمرة، حتى إذا عرفتهم خرج رجل من بيني وبينهم فقال: هلم فقلت: أين ؟ قال: إلى النار والله . قلت : وما شأنهم؟ قال: إنهم ارتدوا بعدك على أدبارهم القهقرى ثم إذا زمرة - فذكر مثله - قال: فلا أراه يخلص منهم إلا مثل همل النعم

"While I was asleep, I saw a group of people (in a dream). I continued to see them until I recognized them. At that point a man came out between them and I and he said (to them), 'Come on.' So I said, 'Where (are you taking them)?' He replied, 'To the Hellfire, by Allaah.' I then said, 'What happened to them?' He replied, 'Verily, they apostated after you, turning their backs in retrogression.' Then another group came and the same thing happened. I do not think there were any sincere ones among them except the likes of a few neglected cattle."

In the two *Saheehs* it is narrated in a *hadeeth* of Ibn 'Abbaas that the Prophet (ﷺ) said,

فأقول كما قال العبد الصالح

"I will say just as the righteous servant ('Eesaa, son of Maryam) said,

﴿ وَكُنتُ عَلَيْهِمْ شَهِيدًا مَّا دُمْتُ فِيهِمْ ۖ فَلَمَّا تَوَفَّيْتَنِى كُنتَ أَنتَ ٱلرَّقِيبَ عَلَيْهِمْ ۚ وَأَنتَ عَلَىٰ كُلِّ شَىْءٍ شَهِيدٌ ﴾

'And I was a witness over them while I dwelt amongst them, but when You took me up, You were the Watcher over them; and You are a Witness to all things.' *(Al-Maa'idah (5):117)*"

It is also narrated in the two *Saheehs* that the Prophet said,

ما من مولو د يولد إلا على الفطرة فأبواه يهو دانه أو ينصرانه أو يمجسانه كما تنتج البهيمة بهيمة جمعاء هل تحسون فيها من جدعاء حتى تكونوا أنتم تجدعونها

"There is no child that is born except that it is (born) on the *Fitrah* (Islaamic Monotheism). But its parents make it a Jew, a Christian, or a Magian (fire worshipper). Just as the cow is born as a whole (healthy) calf. Do you notice any mutilation in it until you all come along and mutilate it (branding it, cutting its ears and tails, etc.)?"

Then Abu Hurairah (the narrator) recited the verse,

﴿ فِطْرَتَ ٱللَّهِ ٱلَّتِى فَطَرَ ٱلنَّاسَ عَلَيْهَا ﴾

"Allaah's Fitrah (Islaamic Monotheism) upon which He has created mankind." *Ar-Room (30):30*

(Agreed upon)

It is reported that Huthayfah said,

كان الناس يسألون رسول الله صلى الله عليه و سلم عن الخير وكنت أسأله عن الشر مخافة أن يدركني فقلت يا رسول الله: إنا كنا في جاهلية و شر فجاءنا الله بهذا الخير، فهل بعد هذا الخير من شر؟ قال: نعم. فقلت: وهل بعد ذلك الشر من خير؟ نعم وفيه دخن قلت: وما دخنه؟ قال: قوم يستنون بغير سنتي ويهدون بغير هديي تعرف منهم وتنكر قلت: فهل بعد ذلك الخير من شر؟ قال: نعم فتنة عمياء و دعاة على أبواب جهنم من أجابهم إليها قذفوه فيها، قلنا: يا رسول الله صفهم لنا قال: قوم من جلدتنا ويتكلمون بألسنتنا - قلت : يا رسول الله ما تأمرني إن أدركت ذلك قال: تلزم جماعة المسلمين وإمامهم، قلت: وإن لم يكن جماعة ولا إمام؟ قال: فاعتزل تلك الفرق كلها ولو أن تعض على أصل شجرة حتى يأتيك الموت وأنت على ذلك

"The people used to ask the Messenger of Allaah about the good, but I used to ask him about the evil out of fear that it would overcome me. So I said, 'O Messenger of Allaah! Verily, we were in a state of ignorance and evil. Then Allah brought us this good (i.e. Islaam). Will there be any evil after this good?' He said, 'Yes.' Then I said, 'Will there be any good after that evil?' He said, 'Yes. But there will be *Dakhan* (blemish) in it.' So I said, 'What will its smoke be?' He replied, 'A group of people who will follow a way other than my *Sunnah,* and they will be direct with other than my guidance. You will recognize some things from them and reject (others).' I said, 'Will there be any evil after that good?' He said, 'Yes. A blind *fitnah* (trial, evil) and callers at the gates of Hell. Whoever responds to their call, they will throw them into it (i.e. Hell).' I said, 'O Messenger of Allaah! Describe them to us.' He replied, 'A people from our skin, and they will speak our language.' I then said, 'O Messenger of Allaah! What do you command me (to do) if I reach that (time)?' He said, 'Adhere to the *Jamaa'ah* (community, group) of the Muslims and their *Imaam.*' I said, 'What if there is no Jamaa'ah and no *Imaam?*' He said, 'Then avoid all of those sects even if you have to bite upon the root of a tree until death comes to you while you are in that state.'" Both Al-Bukhaaree and Muslim have recorded this *hadeeth* and Muslim's version adds,

ثم ما ذا؟ قال: يخرج الدجال معه نهر ونار فمن وقع في ناره وجب أجره قلت ثم ما ذا؟ قال: هي قيام الساعة

"Then I said, 'Then what?' The Prophet replied, 'The *Dajjaal* will appear and he will have a river and a fire with him. So whoever falls into his fire will definitely be rewarded (i.e. with good).' So I said, 'Then what?' He replied, 'It will be the establishment of the Hour (i.e. the end of the world).'"

Abu Al-'Aaliyah said, "Learn Islaam. Then once you have learned it, do not turn away from it. You must adhere to the Straight Path, for verily, it is Islaam. And do not move from the Path, not to the right nor to the left. And you must adhere to the *Sunnah* of your Prophet. And beware of these desires (i.e. deviations)." [32]

Notice this statement of Abu Al-'Aaliyah, for indeed it is great. And you should take note of his time in which he was warning against these desires that whoever follows them turns away from Islaam. Also notice his explanation of Islaam and the *Sunnah*, and his fear for the eminent Successors (i.e. the students of the Companions) and their Scholars, that they might leave the *Sunnah* and the Book (the Qur'aan).

---

[32] Meaning, stay away from the desires, and the desires here means the innovations. Beware of them and adhere to the path.

Thus, the meaning of Allaah's statement becomes clear for you, where He says,

﴿إِذْ قَالَ لَهُۥ رَبُّهُۥٓ أَسْلِمْ ۖ قَالَ أَسْلَمْتُ لِرَبِّ ٱلْعَٰلَمِينَ﴾

"When his (Ibraaheem's) Lord said to him, 'Submit!' He (Ibraaheem) said, 'I have submitted myself (as a Muslim) to the Lord of all that exists.'" *Al-Baqarah (2):131*

And His statement,

﴿وَوَصَّىٰ بِهَآ إِبْرَٰهِـۧمُ بَنِيهِ وَيَعْقُوبُ يَٰبَنِىَّ إِنَّ ٱللَّهَ ٱصْطَفَىٰ
لَكُمُ ٱلدِّينَ فَلَا تَمُوتُنَّ إِلَّا وَأَنتُم مُّسْلِمُونَ﴾

"And this (submission to Allaah, Islaam) was enjoined by Ibraaheem (Abraham) upon his sons and by Ya'qoob (Jacob) (saying), 'O my sons! Allaah has chosen for you the (true) religion, then do not die except as Muslims.'" *Al-Baqarah (2):132*

And His saying,

﴿وَمَن يَرْغَبُ عَن مِّلَّةِ إِبْرَٰهِـۧمَ إِلَّا مَن سَفِهَ نَفْسَهُۥ﴾

"And who turns away from the religion of Ibraaheem (Abraham) except him who befools himself?" *Al-Baqarah (2):130*

And there are other evidences (i.e. verses and *ahadeeth*) that are similar to these and they are the major fundamentals that are the foundation of the fundamentals (of Islaam). Yet, the people are heedless of them. By being aware of this basic fundamental, the meaning of the *ahadeeth* that address this matter and other similar *ahadeeth* become clear. However, the person who reads these evidences and similar evidences, and he feels certain that they do not pertain to him, and he thinks that they refer to people that have passed away before, then it is people like him who feel secure against the plan of Allaah. Yet, no one feels safe against the plan of Allaah except the people who are losers.

It has been reported that Ibn Mas'ood said,

خط لنا رسول الله صلى الله عليه و سلم خطا ثم قال: هذا سبيل الله ثم خط خطوطا عن يمينه وعن شماله ثم قال: هذه سبل على كل سبيل منها شيطان يدعو إليه وقرأ: ﴿وَأَنَّ هَٰذَا صِرَٰطِي مُسْتَقِيمًا فَٱتَّبِعُوهُ ۖ وَلَا تَتَّبِعُوا۟ ٱلسُّبُلَ فَتَفَرَّقَ بِكُمْ عَن سَبِيلِهِۦ﴾

"The Messenger of Allaah (ﷺ) drew a line on the ground for us. Then he said, 'This is the Way of Allaah.' Then he drew lines from its right and its left, and he said, 'On every one of these paths there is a devil calling to it.' Then he recited (the verse),

﴿ وَأَنَّ هَٰذَا صِرَٰطِي مُسْتَقِيمًا فَٱتَّبِعُوهُ ۖ وَلَا تَتَّبِعُوا۟ ٱلسُّبُلَ فَتَفَرَّقَ بِكُمْ عَن سَبِيلِهِۦ ﴾

'And verily, this is my Straight Path, so follow it, and follow not (other) paths, for they will separate you away from His Path.' (*Al-An'aam (6):153)*"
(Ahmad and An-Nasaa'ee) [33]

---

[33] And this clarifies that what is obligatory upon the believer is to beware and not be deceived by the great numbers of people. And the believer should be concerned with the *Sunnah* and the proof. He should fear for himself, and he should not feel safe, because Allaah, the Most High, says (the English meaning is),

"Did they then feel secure against the Plan of Allâh. None feels secure from the Plan of Allâh except the people who are the losers." *Al-A'raaf (7):99*

The person should do deeds and strive upon obedience, while he fears and trembles, and he should not feel at ease. Rather, he should beware of the innovations, and beware of the acts of disobedience, and he should follow the people of the truth and walk with them. He should stay away from the people of falsehood and being in their company. This is how the believer is, he is always cautious. Allaah, the Most High, said (the English meaning is),

"Verily, those who believe and do righteous good deeds, they are the best of creatures. Their reward with their Lord is 'Adn (Eden) Paradise (Gardens of Eternity), underneath which rivers flow, they will abide therein forever, Allaah is pleased with them, and they with Him. That is for him who fears his Lord." *Al-Bayyinah (98):7-8*

And Allaah, the Magnificent and Exalted, said (the English meaning is),

"Verily! Those who fear their Lord unseen, theirs will be forgiveness and a great reward." *Al-Mulk (67):12*

And He, Who is free from imperfections, said (the English meaning is),

"So fear them not, but fear Me, if you are (true) believers." *Aal 'Imraan (3):175*

And He, the Most High, said (the English meaning is),

"And for whoever fears the standing before his Lord, he will have two Gardens (in Paradise)." *Ar-Rahmaan (55):46*

So it is obligatory to beware and not feel at ease with the opinion of so-and-so, and the opinion of so-and-so, until you know the proof from the Book and the *Sunnah*.

What has been reported about the strangeness of Islaam and the virtue of the strangers

Allaah says,

﴿ فَلَوْلَا كَانَ مِنَ ٱلْقُرُونِ مِن قَبْلِكُمْ أُو۟لُوا۟ بَقِيَّةٍ يَنْهَوْنَ عَنِ ٱلْفَسَادِ فِى ٱلْأَرْضِ إِلَّا قَلِيلًا مِّمَّنْ أَنجَيْنَا مِنْهُمْ ﴾

"If only there had been among the generations before you persons having wisdom, prohibiting (others) from *Al-Fasaad* (disbelief, polytheism, corruption and crimes) in the earth, except a few of those whom We saved from among them!" *Hood (11):116*

It has been narrated from Abu Hurairah that the Messenger of Allaah (ﷺ) said,

بدأ الإسلام غريباً و سيعود غريباً كما بدأ فطوبى للغرباء

"Islaam began as something strange and it will return to being something strange just as it began. So glad tidings (of a tree called *Toobaa* in Paradise) for the strangers." (Muslim)

Ahmad recorded this *hadeeth* from Ibn Mas'ood in which he mentioned that it was said,

من الغرباء؟ قال: النزاع من القبائل والذين يصلحون إذ فسد الناس

"Who are the strangers?" The Prophet replied, "The *Nuzzaa'* [34] from the tribes and those who are righteous when the people have become corrupt (or wicked)."

At-Tirmidhee recorded from Katheer bin 'Abdillaah, who narrated from his father, who narrated from his grandfather that the Prophet (ﷺ) said,

فطوبى للغرباء الذين يصلحون ما أفسد الناس من سنتي

"So glad tidings (of a tree called *Toobaa* in Paradise) for the strangers. They are those who correct what the people have corrupted of my *Sunnah*."

It is reported that Abu Umayyah said, "I asked Abu Tha'labah, 'What do you say about this verse,

---

[34] *Nuzzaa'* (singular = *Naazi'* and *Nazee'*): A strange person who withdraws from his people and his tribe (or relatives). He stays away from them and is absent from them. In other words *Toobaa* is for those who migrate, and they are those who stay away from their homelands for the sake of Allaah. (Quoted from *An-Nihaayah fee Ghareeb Al-Hadeeth wal-Athar*, by Ibn Al-Atheer, Vol. 5, pg. 41.)

﴿ يَٰٓأَيُّهَا ٱلَّذِينَ ءَامَنُواْ عَلَيۡكُمۡ أَنفُسَكُمۡۖ لَا يَضُرُّكُم مَّن ضَلَّ إِذَا ٱهۡتَدَيۡتُمۡ ﴾

'O you who believe! Take care of your own selves. If you follow the (right) guidance no hurt can come to you from those who are in error.' *Al-Maa'idah (5):105*

He said, 'By Allaah! Indeed you have asked one who knows about it. I asked the Messenger of Allaah (about it) and he said,

بل ائتمروا بالمعروف وتناهوا عن المنكر حتى إذا رأيتم شحا مطاعاً وهوى متبعا، و دنيا مؤثرة، وإعجاب كل ذي رأي برأيه، فعليك بنفسك، و دع عنك العوام، فإن من ورائكم أياماً الصابر فيهن مثل القابض على الجمر، للعامل فيهن أجر خمسين رجلا يعملون مثل عملكم قلنا: منا أم منهم؟ قال: بل منكم

"Rather (it means), command each other to do good and forbid each other from evil until you see greediness that is obeyed, desires being followed, worldliness being preferred, and every person who has an opinion being pleased with his own opinion. Then (at that time) take care of your ownself and leave the common people alone (i.e. avoid them). For verily, after you all, there will be days when the person who is patient during them will be like someone holding a burning coal (in his hand). The one who works (righteous) deeds in those days will have the reward of fifty men who do deeds like your deeds.' We said, '(Fifty men) from them or from us?' He replied, 'Nay, from you.'" [35] (Abu Daawood and At-Tirmidhee)

---

[35] This contains the encouragement to be steadfast and upright in strangeness, and that it is necessary for the believer to stand firm, and be zealous upon being upright when this strangeness happens among the people (regarding Islaam). He should not be deceived by the numerous amount of those who are upon the way of destruction. For this reason, the Prophet (ﷺ) said in the authentic *hadeeth* when As-Siddeeq (Abu Bakr) recited this verse (the English meaning is),

"O you who believe! Take care of your ownselves. If you follow the right guidance and enjoin what is right and forbid what is wrong, no hurt can come to you from those who are in error." *Al-Maa'idah (5):105*

He said that the Prophet (ﷺ) said, **"Verily the people, when they see the evil and they do not oppose it, it is likely that Allaah will overcome them with His punishment."**

And His statement (the English meaning is),

"If you follow the right guidance and enjoin what is right and forbid what is wrong, no hurt can come to you from those who are in error." *Al-Maa'idah (5):105*

From the right guidance is commanding the good. And the person who is misguided will not harm the people if they stand firm, and command the good and forbid the evil. Some people think that if they adhere to right guidance this means when the person performs the personal acts of obedience (i.e. only concerning himself), and this is a mistake. Also from the right guidance is commanding the good and forbidding evil. This is from the things that bring

Ibn Wadhdhaah reported a *hadeeth* having the same meaning from Ibn 'Umar. Its wording is that the Prophet (ﷺ) said,

---

about right guidance. For this reason As-Siddeeq gave a sermon to the people when he became the leader, and he said, "Verily you all recite this verse and you put it in other than its proper place (the English meaning is),

"O you who believe! Take care of your ownselves. If you follow the right guidance and enjoin what is right and forbid what is wrong no hurt can come to you from those who are in error." *Al-Maa'idah (5):105*

And verily I heard the Messenger of Allaah (ﷺ) saying, '**Verily the people, if they see an evil and they do not oppose it, it is likely that Allaah will overcome them with His punishment.**'" And thus it is in this verse. He (ﷺ) went on to say, **"Rather, command each other with good, and forbid one another from evil until you see stinginess being obeyed, and desires being followed, and worldly things being preferred, and each person with an opinion being amazed with his opinion (i.e. thinking highly of it). Then you must stick to being concerned about your ownself personally and leave off the common folk. For verily there will come after you days in which the patient person in those days will be like someone who holds hot coals in his hand."** Allaah is the One Whose help is sought. These people are the strangers. They are those who are righteous when the people become corrupt, and they set right what the people have corrupted. They do this by commanding the good and forbidding the evil. They adhere to the Qur'aan when the people abandon it. **"Islaam began as something strange and it will return to being something strange just as it began. So glad tidings (of a tree called *Toobaa* in Paradise) for the strangers."** So the strangers are the people of righteousness, and standing firmly upon the truth, and carrying out the commands (of Islaam), and calling to Allaah when the time becomes corrupt and its people change (to evil).

إن من بعدكم أياما للصابر فيها المتمسك بدينه مثل ما أنتم
عليه اليوم، له أجر خمسين منكم

"Verily, after you all there will be days in which the one who is patient during them, adhering to his religion (Islaam) like what you all are upon today (i.e. in the companions' time), he will have the reward of fifty of you."

Then he (Ibn Wadhdhaah) said, "Muhammad bin Sa'eed informed us that Asad informed them that Sufyaan bin 'Uyainah narrated from Aslam Al-Basree, who reported from Sa'eed, the brother of Al-Hasan, who said that the Prophet (ﷺ) said,

إنكم اليوم على بينة من ربكم، تأمرون بالمعروف وتنهون
عن المنكر وتجاهدون في سبيل الله، ولم يظهر فيكم
السكرتان: سكرة الجهل، و سكرة حب العيش،
و ستحولون عن ذلك، فالمتمسك يومئذ بالكتاب والسنة
له أجر خمسين قيل: منهم؟ قال: بل منكم

'Verily, today you all are upon clear guidance from your Lord. You command the good, forbid the evil, and you make *Jihaad* in the Way of Allaah. Also, the two intoxications have not appeared among you: the intoxication of ignorance, and the intoxication of the love of life. But you all are going to change from that (which you are on now). So whoever adheres to the Book (the Qur'aan) and the *Sunnah* on that day (i.e. in those times) then he will have the reward of fifty.' It was said, 'Fifty of them?' He replied, 'Nay, from you.'"

This *hadeeth* also has a chain of narration from Al-Ma'aafiree who said that the Messenger of Allaah said,

طوبى للغرباء، الذين يتمسكون بالكتاب حين يترك،
ويعملون بالسنة حين تطفأ

"*Toobaa* (a huge tree in Paradise) is for the strangers. They are those who adhere to the Book (the Qur'aan) when it will be abandoned, and act according to the *Sunnah* when it will be extinguished."

The warning against innovations [36]

[36] And this contains a warning against innovations, and that what is obligatory upon the people of Islaam is to beware of them. For this reason the Prophet (ﷺ) warned against them when he gave the Companions an intense admonition. It caused their eyes to water with tears and their hearts to tremble. We (the Companions) said, "O Messenger of Allaah, it is as if this is a farewell sermon, so advise us." He said, **"I advise you to fear Allaah, the Mighty and Majestic, and to listen and obey."** This means to obey those in authority. **"Even if a slave is made the leader over you. And indeed, whoever amongst you lives (long), he will see many differences. Therefore, you must adhere to my *Sunnah* and the *Sunnah* of the rightly guided *Khulafaa'* (succeeding rulers). Bite upon it (the *Sunnah*) with the molar teeth (i.e. cling steadfastly to it) and avoid the newly introduced matters. For verily, every innovation is a misguidance."** So what is obligatory upon the people of Islaam is that they stick to what Allaah legislated of acts of worship, and that they beware of what people introduce of innovations. For this reason Huthayfah said, **"Every act of worship that was not done by the Companions of Muhammad, then you don't do it either, for verily the first (generation) did not leave any statement for the latter (generation)."** Because the Companions made things clear, and they asked their Prophet about everything. So you must follow them and traverse upon their methodology.

And when 'Abdullaah ibn Mas'ood saw some people in the *masjid*, and each circle in the *masjid* had one person in it who was saying, "Glorify Allaah like this," and "count it this many times and that many times," and they would count their glorification with pebbles. 'Abdullaah said, "Verily you all are upon a religion that is either more rightly guided than the religion of Muhammad, or you have opened a door of misguidance. So count your sins, for I guarantee that nothing will be lost from your good deeds (if you do so instead of this)." This is from the innovations in their breaking up into groups, with each group having a person saying, "Do such-and-such." For verily all that is obligatory is to advise and to remind each other of Allaah. This is by saying, "Allaah said, and the Messenger said." This is what is obligatory. But in reference to them making circles and saying, "Count your good deeds. Take the pebbles and count O so-and-so!" This is from that which the people have introduced of the innovations. And for this reason the Prophet (ﷺ) said in his sermon, "**Thus to proceed. For verily the best speech is the Book of Allaah. And the best guidance is the guidance of Muhammad (ﷺ). And the worst of the affairs are the newly introduced matters. And every newly introduced matter is an innovation (*Bid'ah*), and every innovation is a misguidance."** So what the people have introduced of things that bring one nearer to Allaah (as they claim), then those things are from the innovations. So the innovations are those things which they believe will bring them closer (to Allaah). So that which people do seeking with it to draw nearer to Allaah, from that which has not been legislated, then these are innovations. So therefore it is obligatory to beware of innovations. And there is no categorizing it. Rather, every innovation is misguidance.

In reference to the statement of some people that innovation is divided into five categories, then this an erroneous statement from whoever says it. And what is correct is that every innovation is misguidance. And innovation is something that the people use to draw near to Allaah, but Allaah did not legislate it. For example, like what these people did in the time of Ibn Mas'ood, and like the innovation of celebrating birthdays, and the innovation of building structures over the graves, and putting up tombstones and writing on them. All of this is from that which the people have innovated from the innovations. So what is obligatory is to be careful, be careful of this, and that the believer restricts himself to what Allaah has legislated, and what the Companions of the Prophet (ﷺ) traversed upon in the acts of worship. And the believer must beware of adding anything to what Allaah, the Majestic and Exalted, has legislated. Allaah, the Most High, said (the English meaning is):

> **"This day, I have perfected your religion for you."** *Al-Maa'idah (5):3*

So Allaah completed the *Deen*, so it is not for anyone to add anything to it.

This is the end of the blessed explanation, and all praise is due to Allaah, the Lord of all that exists.

Al-'Irbaadh bin Saariyah said,

وعظنا رسول الله صلى الله عليه و سلم موعظة بليغة، قلنا: يا رسول الله كأنها موعظة مودع فأوصنا قال: أوصيكم بتقوى الله عز وجل، والسمع والطاعة، وإن أمر عليكم عبد، وإنه من يعش منكم فسيرى اختلافا كثيرا، فعليكم بسنتي و سنة الخلفاء الراشدين المهديين، عضوا عليها بالنواجذ، وإياكم ومحدثات الأمور، فإن كل بدعة ضلالة

"The Messenger of Allaah (ﷺ) admonished us with an intense sermon. So we said, 'O Messenger of Allaah! It is as if this is a farewell sermon, so advise us.' He said, 'I advise you to fear Allaah, the Mighty and Majestic, and to listen and obey, even if a slave is made the leader over you. And indeed, whoever amongst you lives (long), he will see many differences. Therefore, you must adhere to my *Sunnah* and the *Sunnah* of the rightly guided *Khulafaa'* (succeeding rulers). Bite upon it (the *Sunnah*) with the molar teeth (i.e. cling steadfastly to it) and avoid the newly introduced matters. For verily, every innovation is a misguidance.'" (At-Tirmidhee, who said that it is a good and authentic *hadeeth*.)

It is narrated that Huthayfah said, "Every act of worship that the Companions of Muhammad were not performing then you all (the latter generations) should not perform it either. For indeed the first (generation) has not left any statement for the last (generations). So fear Allaah O community of reciters, and take the path of those who were before you." (Abu Daawood)

Ad-Daarimee said that Al-Hakim bin Al-Mubaarak told them that 'Amr bin Yahyaa told them that he heard his father narrating from his father that he said, "We were sitting at the door of 'Abdullaah bin Mas'ood before the morning prayer so that when he came out we could walk with him to the *masjid*. Then Abu Moosaa Al-Ash'aree came to us and said, 'Has Abu 'Abdir-Rahmaan come out yet?' We said, 'No.' So he sat with us. Then when he (Ibn Mas'ood) came out, Abu Moosaa said, 'O Abu 'Abdir-Rahmaan! Verily, I saw in the *masjid* something that I disapproved of and I, all praise is due to Allaah, didn't see other than good.' Ibn Mas'ood said, 'What was it?' He said, 'If you live, you will see it.'

Then he continued, 'I saw people sitting in circles in the *masjid* waiting for the prayer. In every circle there was a man (leading the others) and the people had pebbles in their hands. So the man (who was leading them) would say: Say Allaah is Most Great (*Allaahu Akbar*) one hundred times! So the people would say *Allaahu Akbar* one hundred times. Then the man would say: Say there is no deity worthy of worship except Allaah (*Laa Ilaaha Illa Allaah*) one hundred times! So the people would say *Laa Ilaaha Illa Allaah* one hundred times. Then the man would say: Glorify Allaah (*Subhaan Allaah*) one hundred times! So the people would say *Subhaan Allaah* one hundred times.'

Then Ibn Mas'ood said, 'So what did you say to them?' Abu Moosaa said, 'I did not say anything to them. I'm waiting to see what you say.' Ibn Mas'ood said, 'Why didn't you command them to count their sins and guarantee them that none of their good deeds would be lost (if they did that instead)?' Then he went until he came to one of the circles and said, 'What is this?' They said to him, 'These are stones that we are using to count the *Takbeer* (Allaah's Greatness), *Tahleel* (declare Allaah's Oneness), and *Tasbeeh* (glorification of Allaah).'

He then said, 'Count your sins, for I guarantee that nothing will be lost of your good deeds (if you do so instead of this). Woe unto you O *Ummah* (followers, nation) of Muhammad! You are so quick in your destruction! Here are the Companions of your Prophet in great abundance (i.e. still alive), here are his clothes that have not yet deteriorated, and here are his utensils and they are not even broken yet. By Him in Whose Hand is my soul, verily you all are upon a religion that is either more rightly guided than the religion of Muhammad, or you have opened a door of misguidance.' They said, 'By Allaah, O Abu 'Abdir-Rahmaan, we only intended good.' He replied, 'How many people intend good but do not achieve it? Verily, the Messenger of Allaah (ﷺ) told us that some people will recite the Qur'aan and it will not go past their throats. By Allaah! Most of them will probably be from you all.'"

'Amr bin Salamah said, "We saw most of those people fighting against us on the Day of the Battle of Nahrawaan with the *Khawaarij*."

This is the end of what has been made easy (by Allaah).

Allaah is the One Who is sought for help and upon Him one puts his trust. May Allaah mention our leader Muhammad among His noble gathering of Angels and may He bestow peace and blessing upon him, and his family and all of his Companions.